For Mum, who gave me roots, and for Dad, who has the wisdom of trees – R. S.
For Axel and his apple trees, with all my love – H. C.

Barefoot Books
124 Walcot Street
Bath BA1 5BG

First published in Great Britain in 2003 by Barefoot Books Ltd
This paperback edition published in 2005

This book has been printed on 100% acid-free paper
The illustrations were prepared in watercolour, graphite and collage
on 140lb Bockingford paper
Design by Jennie Hoare, Bradford on Avon
Typeset in 12pt Minion
Colour separation by Bright Arts, Singapore
Printed and bound in China by Printplus Ltd

Paperback ISBN 1-84148-806-2

British Cataloguing-in-Publication Data: a catalogue record for this book
is available from the British Library

5 7 9 8 6 4

A FOREST OF STORIES

MAGICAL TREE TALES FROM AROUND THE WORLD

retold by Rina Singh • illustrated by Helen Cann

Barefoot Books
Celebrating Art and Story

CONTENTS

INTRODUCTION

Trees are the oldest living things on earth. They were here long before man appeared on this planet. They live for centuries and some are known to date back two thousand years or more. They are, in a sense, our living ancestors.

Trees are also here with us now. We have a direct relationship with them — an unfair alliance, in which we accept a multitude of gifts from them and offer nothing in return. We nourish ourselves with the fruit they provide, and we use their wood to make our homes. We plant them in our gardens and parks, and we heal ourselves with the medicines they give us. We have both creatively and selfishly put every part of them to use, and yet they make no demands on us. They stand still, holding the soil in place, controlling floods and providing homes to countless animals.

We are cutting down more and more trees, for short-term commercial gain. It is a frightening thought that if we continue cutting them down at this rate, not only will many plants and animals become extinct, but our own very survival will be at risk. We can no longer afford to be indifferent to trees or ignorant about them. They are too precious.

There is a New Guinean saying, 'Our forests are a gift from our ancestors which must be passed on to our children.' Like our ancestors, trees are worthy of our respect. As our contemporaries, they have a right to co-exist with us in harmony. And, like our children, trees deserve our love.

Trees have held a special place in the world's folklore. This book is not only a portrait of seven unique trees but it is a celebration of all the trees growing in the world. I hope the book shows you some of the magic of trees and brings you a bit closer to them as you journey through the pages.

Rina Singh

The Weeping Cypress is a native of China
and forms extensive forests along the Yangtze River.

The tree has projecting branches,
and the smaller ones on the sides hang down,
giving the tree a very graceful look.

The twigs have a reddish-brown colour.

The timber is of good quality
and is used to build houses and boats.

The tree is not very hardy so cultivation is restricted to warmer areas.

THE CYPRESS TREE
Chinese

Long ago, in a village on the banks of the Yangtze River, lived a merchant named Li Jian. He sold spices for a living and had a temper as fiery as his wares. Customers who had the courage to query his prices were immediately sent packing, and woe to any stranger who stopped at his house to ask for directions or to borrow a bowl of rice. Li had two dogs with fierce eyes and square heads, and he would threaten to set them on any one who approached his house. Li's wife disapproved of his behaviour, but there was little she could do about it.

Li lived in a small house by the side of the road. It had a pagoda roof, a narrow courtyard at the front, and a vegetable garden at the back. Outside his house, at the side of the road, grew a great cypress tree, which he claimed had been planted by his great-grandfather. It was a tall, graceful tree, with the bigger branches projecting towards the sky and the smaller ones hanging down towards the earth. The twigs were a beautiful reddish-brown colour. Li was very proud of his tree because it blocked out the afternoon sun and brought shade to his sitting room on hot summer days.

One day, after finishing his dinner of steamed rice, noodles and fish, Li stepped out into his courtyard to enjoy the breeze. He was dismayed to see a poor, bedraggled pedlar taking a nap under his tree. How dare anyone trespass on his property, he thought to himself.

'Why should anyone else enjoy the shade of my tree?' he shouted loudly and stomped towards the pedlar. He shook him rudely and ordered him to leave. The poor pedlar was dazed by the sudden awakening, and wanted to know what he had done to deserve such treatment.

'You were sleeping in the shade of my tree!' cried Li, angrily.

'I beg your pardon, sir,' said the pedlar most humbly. 'I thought trees belonged to everyone — and besides, this one is on public property.' The pedlar looked around to make sure that he was committing no crime.

'That may be so, but the tree belongs to me, and no one else can enjoy it,' Li replied, becoming angrier by the minute. The dogs trotted up behind him and awaited orders from their master. The pedlar took one look at their mean eyes, scrambled for his wares and scurried away. The merchant watched him leave, still cursing him under his breath.

A few days later, the pedlar passed by the tree and briefly paused to blush from the insults he had endured under it. He was startled to hear the branches whisper something into his ears. He walked away, pleased with the idea the tree had planted in his head.

Many days later, upon returning from his shop, Li found the same pedlar again sleeping under his tree.

'How dare you return,' he hollered. 'Leave immediately or I will set my dogs upon you!'

'Pardon me, sir,' said the pedlar, most respectfully, 'but I have a proposition for you.'

A proposition, thought Li. Was the man mad?

'And what might that be?' he asked, with the last bit of his patience.

'I would like to buy the shade of your tree,' said the pedlar, with a straight face.

'Buy the shade of my tree?' repeated Li. The pedlar nodded.

The merchant had never heard of anyone buying the shade of a tree. It struck him as odd, but his curiosity got the better of him.

'How much?' he asked, suspiciously.

'Twenty-five pieces of gold,' said the pedlar, unwrapping a ragged piece of cloth to show his treasure.

'Twenty-five pieces of gold!' repeated Li, trying not to show his greed.

And so it was settled. For twenty-five pieces of gold the pedlar could enjoy the shade of the tree whenever he wanted. Before he handed over the money, however, the pedlar insisted on drawing up a deed of sale, which recorded the details of the transaction. Li willingly accompanied him to the judge, who wrote out three copies of the deed. Li was delighted to have struck such a clever bargain and the pedlar went away, humming to himself.

Day after day, the pedlar returned to enjoy the shade. Some days he took a nap and on others he sat wrapping his wares in little pouches. One

day, he brought some friends, whose clothes were as threadbare as his own. They sat under the tree playing a game of cards. It was a hot summer's day, and by afternoon the shade had moved into Li's sitting room. The pedlar and his friends picked up their game and their belongings and moved inside the house. Li's wife, who had been tending her vegetable garden at the back, heard loud laughter coming from inside the house. She came running in, only to find strange, unkempt men sprawled in her sitting room.

'What is the meaning of this?' asked the woman, totally bewildered.

'You had better ask your husband,' chuckled the pedlar, and continued to contemplate what card to play next. Li's wife rushed out of the house and sent a message to him.

When Li came home, he was speechless with rage. When he found his voice, he yelled, 'Get out of my house, you rogues!'

'Wait a minute!' said the pedlar, pulling the deed of sale from his pocket and waving it in Li's face. 'It's my shade, remember? I go where it goes, and right now it happens to be in your sitting room.' His friends tried to muffle their chuckles.

This was preposterous. Panic-stricken, Li marched to the judge's house and demanded justice. The judge looked at the deed and shook his head at Li's foolishness. There was nothing to be done. The deed could not be annulled without the consent of both parties. Li walked slowly back home wondering what to do. At last he had an idea: he would buy back the shade.

'That's not possible!' said the pedlar.

'Why not?' asked Li, nervously.

'Because the price has just gone up and I don't think that you can afford it,' said the pedlar.

'I will give you fifty pieces of gold,' offered Li, beads of sweat forming on his forehead.

'Two hundred,' said the pedlar firmly, and his friends nodded in approval.

'This is robbery!' cried Li, as he emptied out his treasure chest to get rid of the pedlar.

The pedlar was delighted with his fortune. It is believed that he used some of the gold to open a teashop in the village, where he served the choicest teas. And surely, there was always a table for his friends who gathered to play cards. The matchmaker even found the pedlar a wife, and he lived a comfortable, happy life. As for Li Jian, he was left with nothing. Like his money, his wife left him too. He lived with his miserable dogs and cursed the day that he had set eyes on the pedlar. But from that day on, he never stopped anyone from enjoying the shade of the great cypress tree.

The kapok tree is the most majestic tree in the forests of Central America.

It was the sacred tree of the Mayans.

It can grow enormous, reaching more than sixty metres in height.
The crown of the tree towers above the forest
and looks like an umbrella.

The kapok tree is also called the silk-cotton tree.

The fibre from its seeds was used for stuffing mattresses.

In the dry season, it bears white flowers, which have an unpleasant smell.

The nectar of the blossoms is sought after by bats.

THE KAPOK TREE
Guatemalan

Many years ago, in a rainforest in Guatemala, there grew a great kapok tree. The forest was so thick that once you were in it you couldn't see the sky. All you could see were trees, many trees, and the forest floor, which was deep in dead, wet leaves.

There were other kapok trees in the forest, too, but none of them was as majestic as this one. It was the tallest and the largest tree in the forest. It was so tall that you couldn't see the top of it because it poked right through the canopy to tower over the rainforest like a giant umbrella. It was so enormous that the base itself was about twenty hugs round and its branches seemed to reach the sky.

The people in that part of the world believed that the spirits of the dead travelled through the branches of this tree to the heavens. There were rumours of other things happening, too. People spoke in whispers about the souls who never made it to the heavens and remained trapped in the great kapok's trunk. The tormented spirits became gnarled and twisted in its branches. The rainforest was both haunted and magical.

In Choco Machacas, a village on the edge of the rainforest, people said that if men tried to enter the forest they might never come back. The lucky ones who did return brought back wild flowers and fruit that had magical powers to cure ailments. Some even brought back ants, which

when thrown on wounds which seemed to be incurable, snapped them shut and healed them.

In Choco Machacas lived a young girl named Rio. She was as beautiful as the river she was named after. Her eyes were deep as the waters of the river and the young men were mesmerised. They tried to please her with gifts and offered to marry her but she didn't seem to be in any great hurry to settle down. One of her admirers, Vidal, refused to be put off, and asked her time and time again what he could do to prove his love.

One day, when she was returning to her hut, he stopped her and said, 'Stop playing with my heart, Rio. You know it belongs to you. What do I have to do to prove it to you?'

Startled by his sudden appearance, she said the first thing that came into her mind.

'Go to the rainforest and find the great kapok tree and bring me eighteen fruits and eighteen flowers.'

All the girls dreamed of washing in the nectar from the blossom and stuffing the seeds of the fruit into their pillows. The nectar promised beautiful skin, and the seeds were said to bring splendid dreams.

She expected Vidal to hesitate; she thought he would be afraid of the rainforest and turn away like the other young men, but Vidal stood there like a tree.

'In a month's time,' she added, 'the rains will stop and the tree will blossom and bear fruit. I warn you: the smell from the blossom is so horrible that it is

14

unbearable, but if you bring me the flowers and the fruit despite this, I will be yours.'

After she had said this, Rio went into her hut. Vidal stood outside, wondering why Rio needed to wash in the nectar from the blossom, as she was already so beautiful. But if that's what she wanted, that's what he would get her. He had just turned to go when Rio came out of the hut again and added a warning: 'Beware of the bats, Vidal!'

Vidal went away and waited for the rains to stop. The rain continued to pour down through the nights and days and he grew restless.

His friends warned him, 'Don't go, Vidal. The forest will swallow you.' The elders cautioned him, 'The spirits in the tree will never let you return.'

But Vidal had only one thing on his mind — to marry Rio. One morning he woke up and saw a clear sky, without a single cloud. He took a bag made of hemp and began his walk to the rainforest. As he entered it he could hear the toucans and the macaws up in the canopy. Then, for a few moments, the rainforest became still. The spider monkeys and the anteaters watched him with suspicion. The tree snakes, the sloths and the frogs all stopped what they were doing to watch the intruder. When they saw that he carried no blowgun and showed no interest in hurting them, they ignored him and continued with their activities. There was no path in the rainforest so no

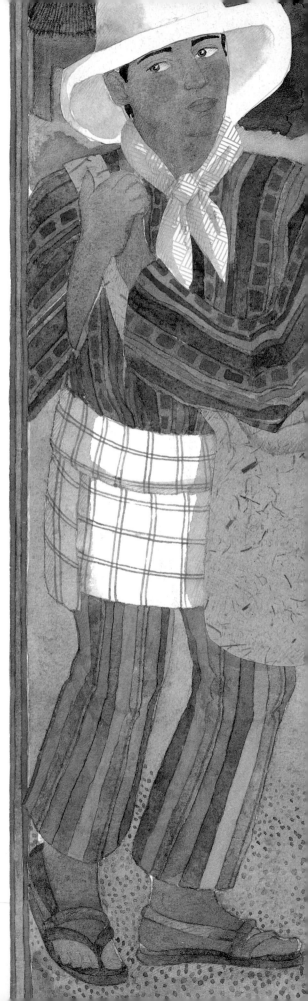

matter how much he struggled through the trees he seemed to get nowhere. After hours and hours, he at last found himself in front of a giant tree. He looked up and trembled. It was indeed the kapok tree for which he was searching. He felt as if he was in the presence of a great spirit. He looked up again and saw that the sun still streaked through the gaps in the trees. The tree would not blossom till sunset, and he was tired from all the walking and the heat. He put the bag under his head and slept.

An awful stench and screeching noises woke him, and he watched in awe as hundreds of bats sucked the nectar of the white blossoms. The tree snakes had disguised themselves as vines and lay in wait to seize the bats. Vidal crouched on the forest floor. He opened his bag and began to

collect only the fruit capsules and the flowers that had fallen on to the forest floor.

'Stop! You must leave the forest.'

Vidal looked around to see who had spoken to him. He could see nothing but the snakes and the bats. He must be imagining that he had heard something, he told himself, or maybe the heat had gone to his head. He bent down quickly to pick up more flowers as the bats circled his head. The bats wouldn't kill him — they rarely attacked humans, he reasoned to himself. And the spirits were trapped inside the trunk. What could they possibly do? But he felt his legs becoming heavy and he could barely move them. In a panic, he dropped the bag and held on to his legs. To his relief, he felt blood circulating in them again. He felt slightly dizzy, so he leaned against the tree to steady himself. Then he picked up the bag again and began counting the fruit — five, six, seven. He wanted to get out of the forest as fast as he could.

His legs began to feel heavy again. He tried to shake them but they seemed to be rooted to the forest floor. This must be the work of the spirits in the tree.

'Let me go!' he begged them.

'Drop the bag and leave,' said the spirits. 'This is your last chance. Walk away from the forest. We forbid you to take any flowers or fruit with you.'

But Vidal couldn't leave and go back to face Rio without the gifts he had promised her. Better to perish

18

in the rainforest than to fail his beloved. He held on to the bag even tighter and his legs grew harder.

'Let me go!' he pleaded.

The tree spirits spoke no more but now Vidal could not move. He looked down and saw, in horror, that his lower body had turned into bark and that slowly his arms were turning into vines. The bag fell to the ground, spilling the blossoms and fruit.

Back in the village, rumours spread that the tree spirits had devoured Vidal. When Rio heard of his sacrifice, she was heart-broken. How could she have been unfair to the one who loved her so deeply? Without whispering as much as a word to anyone, she went into the rainforest, searching for him. She walked and walked for a day and a night, until at last she found herself in front of the great kapok tree. When she looked up, she too trembled. She had never seen anything so magnificent. Then her eyes fell on Vidal, turned into wood. Rio fell on her knees and wept. She begged the tree spirits to release him and hold her captive instead.

Perhaps her tears or maybe her love touched the tree spirits, for gradually, wood turned back into flesh and Vidal came to life.

Rio cried with joy and together they made their way out of the rainforest — but only after they had hugged the kapok tree and vowed to be true to each other for the rest of their lives.

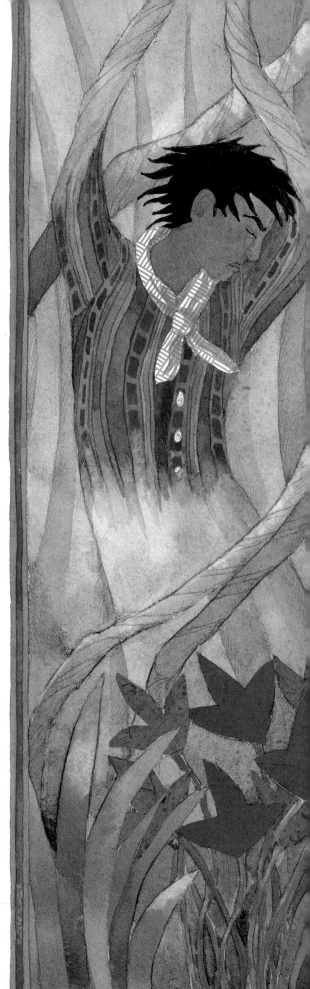

The chestnut tree typically grows up to a height of ten metres and has a rounded crown.

It has dark green leaves and bears tiny clustered flowers.

It yields nuts enclosed in brown prickly husks.

Originally considered food for horses, these nuts are now a luxury item.

The chestnut tree is also a valuable source of timber.

THE CHESTNUT TREE
Japanese

In the days when princes ruled the regions of Japan, there lived a poor fisherman named Saburo. He lived in a small coastal village with his wife, Hana, and their beautiful little daughter, Aiko. His cottage was plain and poor outside — beaten by many years of sun and rain — and almost bare inside. Some of the wooden planks were not properly nailed together, and on windy nights the house seemed to tremble along with the family who lived in it.

During the fishing season, Hana woke up early to prepare rice balls for Saburo, who would take his boat out into the bay and remain there until evening, casting his nets for fish. Hana and Aiko would wait anxiously for his return. Occasionally, when Saburo brought home a big catch, Hana would serve thick soup with slivers of real fish instead of the watery broth they had every day, and she would even make rice cakes for Aiko. These special meals with her mother and father were Aiko's favourite times of all. She loved her parents dearly.

The years passed and Aiko grew into a beautiful girl, with such gentle manners that the neighbours could not help but notice.

One day, during the fishing season, Saburo set out as usual. The sky was overcast and the clouds looked dark and threatening. As the day grew stormier, and Saburo did not return, Hana and Aiko became worried.

The wind howled all night, and still Saburo did not return. It was not until the next day that Hana and Aiko learned that Saburo had been drowned in an accident. His boat had been struck by a large fishing vessel and sunk.

That day, Hana and Aiko's lives changed for ever. The villagers helped them through their grief, bringing small trays of food and bowls of rice, for they were kind people and knew misfortune could hit anyone. But it is hard to be generous when you are poor yourself and have little to spare.

After their savings were gone, Aiko could no longer bear to see her mother grow pale with hunger. 'I am going to look for work in the town,' she announced. Despite her mother's objections, she walked for an hour to the nearest town, Uchimira. She knocked on many doors to offer her services as a servant but most of the homes already had help. Finally, Aiko came to a rich household, where she found employment as a maidservant. The work was long and hard. Aiko's hands became ragged and sore as she cleaned and scoured, hauled wood and swept floors. Often she found her eyes closing from tiredness as she worked. And because she chose to walk home every day to be with her mother, instead of living with the mistress like the other servant girls, she became more and more exhausted.

Halfway between the village and town, Aiko would often stop to rest by a stately chestnut tree. The moment she saw the tree, Aiko felt a sense of relief, for she knew she had completed much of her journey. She would sit by the tree, stroking its brownish-grey bark and removing twigs stuck to its trunk. Later she got into the habit of talking to the tree about her own life, and the grief of her aging mother. She felt great comfort in the presence of the tree, and grew to love it in all its seasons. In summer, she brought home tiny clustered flowers for her mother. In autumn, she saw the dark green leaves turn to a pretty pale yellow colour, and she picked up the prickly fruits with delicious nuts inside. After her secret meetings with the tree, Aiko always felt a little better. It was as if the tree imparted its strength to her and the journey seemed to pass more quickly. The years passed and Aiko grew into a young woman.

One evening, as she was returning to her village, Aiko sat down to rest by the chestnut tree. She felt a sense of sadness in the air and pressed herself closer to her old friend for comfort. Suddenly, she heard a strange voice coming from above her, as if from the tree.

'Aiko, my child,' the voice said. 'The time has come for us to part. The prince has given orders to cut me down. Now listen carefully. A ship will be made out of me. In a few months' time that ship will be launched from your village. I will not move till you come and hug me like you do every day and say, "I am Aiko, your friend."'

Aiko looked up. Trees don't talk, she reasoned to herself. But from where else could the voice have come? Perhaps she was too tired and was imagining things. But somehow, she felt the tree had shared its sorrow with her for the first time. Confused and saddened, Aiko hurried home in the darkness.

The next day, she stopped by the tree and nothing seemed to have changed, so she shared her secret with the tree. 'I had a bad dream,' she said. 'I dreamed that the prince gave orders to cut you down. I could not bear it if they took you away.' And she hugged the tree. The breeze rustled through the leaves and Aiko went home.

A few days later, when Aiko was returning to the village, she got caught in a sudden rainstorm. The rainy season was the hardest to bear. It was a season of chill and gloom. As the thunder clapped, Aiko ran to take shelter under the thick foliage of the chestnut tree. To her horror, it was gone. Her tree was gone. Holding her hands to her mouth, she ran to where the tree had stood. As the rain poured down around her, Aiko stroked the stump and cried as if a dear friend had been taken away. It was no dream after all. The tree *had* spoken to her. Aiko gathered some dead leaves to remind her of her friendship, and walked home through the rain, weary and saddened to her core.

Aiko's walk to and from work was never the same. As the days wore on, she grew pale and weak. The neighbours no longer spoke of her beauty or her graceful manners. It seemed to them as if the Aiko they once knew had disappeared.

One morning, as Aiko set off for Uchimira, she noticed there was a great bustle in the village. A large ship had arrived during the night, and preparations were in progress for its launch into the sea. With all the excitement going on, Aiko decided not to go to work. Instead, she watched amazed as villagers crowded on to the shore to see the prince arrive in a royal palanquin for the launch of the ship. He wore a magnificent black kimono, with coats of arms embroidered down the front and sleeves. The villagers bowed in reverence.

Soon it was time for the prince to set sail. And just as the tree had predicted, the ship would not move. Many men tried to push it into the sea but it seemed rooted into the sand. The embarrassed prince addressed his men and the challenge was thrown to the crowd. Many strong fishermen tried their luck but the ship would not yield.

Aiko stood among the crowd, the secret bursting in her heart. 'Let me try!' she said, her face flushing with nervousness. The crowd fell silent. They couldn't believe that they had heard a woman's voice. They all turned their heads to see to whom the voice belonged.

'Why, if it isn't our Aiko!' cried a surprised neighbour, breaking the long, awkward silence. They all loved Aiko, and admired her devotion to her

mother, but what was the girl doing? When they saw the intensity in her eyes, the crowd began to cheer, 'Aiko! Aiko!' She started walking towards the ship. The royal guards jumped angrily to block her way but the prince signalled his men to stay back. This was the most curious thing he had ever seen. The crowd fell silent again and watched Aiko closely, afraid for her.

She went up to the ship and stroked it just as she used to stroke the tree. But nothing happened. Overcome by emotion, Aiko realised she had forgotten to say the words. Sensing the unease of the crowd behind her, she hugged the ship and whispered, 'I am Aiko, your friend.' Slowly, the ship began to glide into the sea. The prince looked on in amazement as the crowd cheered wildly. He signalled to them to be quiet and ordered Aiko to be brought into his presence. He wanted to see the strong woman for himself. Instead, he saw a slender girl, who radiated a quiet beauty.

Aiko bowed deeply before the prince. He asked her the secret of her strength, and Aiko confessed she had none. Then she told him the story of her friendship with the chestnut tree.

'How can I reward you?' asked the prince, unable to stop staring.

Aiko shook her head. She told him she was already rewarded with the memory of a special friendship and tears rolled down her delicate, pale cheeks. It may sound strange, but the prince was enchanted. And stranger still was what happened next. He asked her to marry him in the presence of all the villagers.

A wave of shock went through the crowd at first and then the villagers began to cheer again and congratulated Hana, who was among the crowd. Aiko looked tenderly at the ship and then her eyes searched for her mother. Hana raised her hands to give her blessings and Aiko smiled through her tears.

Her good fortune was indeed a gift of friendship from the chestnut tree.

The Cherry Blossom is an ornamental tree,

cultivated in gardens for its beautiful bark and blossoms.

The rich reddish-burgundy trunk looks like a column.

The wood is strong and is used to make furniture, pillars and cabinets.

In spring, the fragrant white and pale pink flowers

open in great profusion.

THE CHERRY BLOSSOM TREE
Indian

A few thousand years ago, there flourished in India the city of Benares. It sprawled along the banks of the River Ganges and was famous for its many splendid temples, where monkeys wandered in and out as freely as the saffron-robed holy men. In the mornings, the sun worshippers, their bodies smeared with ashes, stood waist-deep in the river, offering their greetings to the rising sun. Outside the temples, the shopkeepers set up stalls of garlands, fruits and sweets, and when the bells rang, people flocked in to sing hymns and chant prayers. Thinkers came to the city searching for the meaning of life, holy men to seek enlightenment, religious leaders to spread their teachings, and ordinary people to wash their sins away in the holy river.

Besides being a holy city, Benares was a prosperous trading centre. It had silk, which few other cities in India could lay claim to. And not just any silk — silk so pure that it was the official fabric of all religious ceremonies. The narrow dusty streets of Benares were lined with shops selling embroidered silks, satins and hand-woven brocades.

At the time, there lived in Benares a wealthy widower and silk merchant named Vishnu. On this particular day, Vishnu's house was bustling with activity. He was getting ready to embark on a journey to Central Asia, where he would sell his luxurious silks. All Vishnu's friends

came to wish him a safe journey, for it was going to be a long one, probably lasting many months. As the friends mingled together and chatted to each other, they soon discovered that Vishnu had not asked any of them to look after his business affairs in his absence. Nor, for that matter, had he trusted them with his property in case anything should happen to him. It was, after all, a dangerous journey. It was not uncommon for bandits to attack the silk merchants as their caravans travelled through the Khyber Pass in the Hindu Kush Mountains. Finally, after much disagreement and speculation, the friends approached Vishnu and asked why he had not entrusted his affairs to anyone. Vishnu surprised them by saying that he had, in fact, appointed someone to look after his business. He had asked Rao Ji.

'You can't mean Rao Ji, the servant who cooks for you?' asked one friend in disbelief. Surely Vishnu hadn't lost his mind?

'Why not?' countered Vishnu. 'Rao Ji has taken good care of me.'

'But he gets paid to take care of you,' replied his friend.

'You shouldn't trust servants with your wealth!' cautioned another friend. 'And besides, a servant cannot be a friend.'

'Not only that,' added another friend, 'Rao Ji is low-caste. He is too poor and lowly to be in charge of such important matters!'

30

But Vishnu would not listen to them. 'Rao Ji's caste does not matter to me. He has been a faithful friend and has taken care of me in sickness. Should anything happen to me, I can't think of anyone who deserves to inherit my earthly possessions more.'

Still the friends were not satisfied with Vishnu's answers. Finally, one of them had an idea. 'Let's go and ask the Buddha,' he said.

Now, everyone knew that the great Buddha just happened to be visiting Benares at the time and that he was the wisest monk of all. Surely, he would have advice for Vishnu and his friends.

So they all set off for the park where the Buddha in his yellow robes sat cross-legged under a tree talking to his followers. Vishnu and his friends bowed in homage. As the Buddha looked at them and smiled, his face and eyes radiated with an inner light. He joined his hands in welcome to the newcomers, and he listened to their predicament. After pondering their problem in silence for a while, the Buddha decided to tell them a story, as he often did to illustrate his sermons:

Long, long ago, there lived a king, whose palace was surrounded by a beautiful garden. In his garden grew a multitude of trees — apples, plums and pears. But none of the trees was as beautiful as the spectacular cherry blossom tree that stood amongst them. This tree had a rich, reddish-brown bark and a

trunk, upright like a pillar, with branches thrusting in every direction. And just like an actor, the cherry blossom tree put on a show every season to dazzle the king. In summer, it was full of energy and was covered with glossy green leaves. In autumn, the leaves changed to a beautiful golden yellow. In winter, when its leaves fell to the ground, the tree still stood upright with pride and solemn dignity. But it was in spring that the spectacle was incomparable. When the tree blossomed and produced beautiful blizzards of pink and white flowers, it made the king's heart quiver. In this tree, the king saw the cycle of life itself, and it was indeed the jewel of his garden.

Everyone at the palace admired the cherry blossom tree so much that no one ever noticed the kusa grass that grew in clumps around it. People trampled upon the plain-looking grass to get to the tree, but never looked down to give it any attention. Truly, the grass was very content with its life, basking in the splendour of its beloved cherry tree. It was never lonely — the grasshoppers adored it, the ladybirds played hide-and-seek in it, and the clever chameleons disguised themselves in it, looking for prey. In the company of the beautiful cherry tree and other friends, the grass was so happy that it did not mind being trampled upon.

Now one day, during the monsoon, the king's servants noticed that the ceiling of the king's bedroom was beginning to cave in. The pillar that held up the ceiling had rotted with age and needed to be replaced. If it was not taken care of immediately, the king would have no place to sleep, and there could be considerable damage to the adjoining rooms as well. The worried king sent his men to search the palace garden for a tree to replace the old pillar. The men measured all the trees but could find only one with a trunk strong enough to do the job. It was the king's favourite, the cherry blossom tree.

'No! No! No!' cried the king. Just entertaining the idea of felling the tree was unbearable to him. He would not hear of it. Once again, he sent out his men in search of a suitable tree, and again they came back with bowed heads. The cherry tree was the only tree that would save the palace. He could not bring himself to give orders for the felling of the tree. It was only when his advisers intervened and reasoned with him that it was after all only a tree and not more important than the palace, did the distraught king reluctantly make the decision. He summoned the royal priest who chanted prayers to the spirit of the tree, and deemed late evening to be the most favourable time to bring it down.

The news spread quickly amongst the tree spirits and that night the garden fell strangely quiet. The spirits of the other trees gathered around the cherry blossom tree, trying to come up with ways to save it.

All the trees were sad, but the kusa grass was inconsolable. It wasn't sure what to do, but it knew that it could not sit back and watch as the tree was demolished. Every creature in the garden was ready to help, too, if only they could think of a plan.

The next day, the axe-men arrived after sunset and started breaking away some of the overhanging branches to make it easier for them to fell the tree. Suddenly, the junior axe-man touched the trunk and screamed.

'The tree has rotted,' he cried.

'What do you mean?' snapped the head axe-man. 'We checked the tree just yesterday.'

'Feel for yourself,' said the junior axe-man, shrinking away in fear. The head axe-man touched the tree. It was soft and slimy to the touch, and looked discoloured. Such deterioration overnight not only puzzled the axe-men but also filled them with fear.

'This tree must be sacred,' proclaimed the head axe-man. 'We do not want to invite the wrath of the tree spirit!' The junior axe-man agreed, and they decided to scour the city parks for another tree before reporting to the king. They returned only after they had selected one. It was not as strong and upright as the cherry blossom tree, but it would have to do.

The king was overjoyed when he heard that his cherry tree would be spared. But his delight soon turned to devastation when he learned that the tree had mysteriously died. Overwhelmed with emotion, the king ran to his garden to mourn his poor tree. But when he arrived, nothing seemed to be wrong. The sun was shining, the birds were singing and the tree looked more beautiful than ever. It was a miracle! The king summoned the royal priest again, but this time to thank the tree spirits with pieces of ceremonial thread and splashes of holy water from the River Ganges. At night, the trees of the garden rejoiced, too, and begged the cherry blossom tree to tell them the secret behind the miracle. Proudly, the cherry tree explained how the kusa grass had rounded up all the chameleons in the garden and told them to drape themselves around its trunk, making it appear soft and slimy. There was great happiness throughout the garden, but the kusa grass was the happiest of all.

When the Buddha had finished his story, he smiled at his visitors. 'It matters not how poor your friends are,' he said, summing up his sermon. 'Choose your friends not for their position in life, not for their riches, but for their love and wisdom.'

The followers nodded in agreement and Vishnu smiled. His friends, however, humbled by the story, agreed that the Buddha had spoken wisely.

The date palm has a slender trunk, which can be spiky or smooth.

The tree can grow up to a height of twenty metres.

The crown has long leaves that are either shaped like feathers or fans.

The palm's uses are many and varied —
for instance, it produces dates, wax, sugar, oil and wine.

Its fibre is used for making mats, brooms and baskets.

It is also prized for its shade and medicinal value.

Wherever it grows in the world, it is also called the tree of life.

THE PALM TREE
Nigerian

There was once a magician, named Yobachi Baba, who lived in a village in southern Nigeria. His hut was on the outskirts of the village, away from the other compounds. There he lived with his son, Ojo, and two pets, a tortoise and a monkey.

Ojo was young but clever. He helped his father to prepare packets of magic substances and to chant spells to drive evil spirits away. The tortoise was old, even older than Yobachi Baba. He was like an elder in the family. The monkey, on the other hand, was young and sprightly and knew how to climb trees. He was trained to bring down special medicinal leaves that could be used to help blind people to see again.

Now Yobachi Baba was no ordinary magician. He had such a fine reputation that people came from far-off villages to seek his help. Women brought their sick children and men came with their problems. If they couldn't find a wife, or if they wanted to break a long spell of bad luck, they would visit the old magician. As was the custom, people came laden with gifts of food — maize and beans, guavas and papayas. Women brought spicy stews: Ojo's favourite was gari, which is made by pounding the roots of the cassava plant. And sometimes, when the chiefs came, they brought more expensive gifts. Fine leopard skins and beautifully embroidered robes hung on the walls of the hut, bearing testimony to

Yobachi Baba's skills as a magician and a master healer. The food and gifts were so plentiful that Yobachi Baba never had to go to the local market-place, and Ojo didn't even know it existed.

One day, during the rainy season, Yobachi Baba fell ill. It was a strange fever that lasted seven days and seven nights. He gave himself medicine after medicine, but could not heal himself. Ojo was beside himself with worry. He could not help his father either, and at the end of the week Yobachi Baba died. Ojo was heartbroken and so were his father's two faithful pets. The villagers came in crowds to mourn Yobachi Baba's death, and brought food for Ojo. But after three days, they suddenly stopped coming. It wasn't as if they didn't care any more — they simply had other things to do with their lives. And soon the food was gone. The tortoise and the monkey looked desperately at Ojo, with hunger rumbling in their bellies.

Ojo knew that he had to do something. First, he decided to send the monkey to steal some food from the village. But the monkey was easily excited, and the villagers soon spotted him and chased him away. Ojo knew it was now up to him and the tortoise to find food. Together, they hatched plan after plan to steal food, but nothing ever seemed to work. At times they found themselves having to run for their lives, and when they actually did manage to steal a little food, the three of them would have to share it, which left them still very hungry.

After a while, they took to wandering about during the day. They roamed through the flat lands and the forest, eating nuts, roots and berries, until one morning they came to the crossing of two roads. Although it was still early, the roads were both very busy, with people approaching from all directions. Everyone was laden with wares to sell, and when they reached the palm-grove that stood near the crossroads,

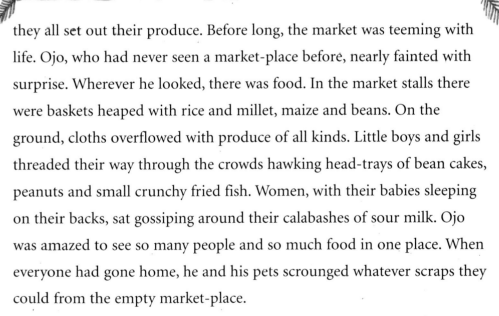

they all set out their produce. Before long, the market was teeming with life. Ojo, who had never seen a market-place before, nearly fainted with surprise. Wherever he looked, there was food. In the market stalls there were baskets heaped with rice and millet, maize and beans. On the ground, cloths overflowed with produce of all kinds. Little boys and girls threaded their way through the crowds hawking head-trays of bean cakes, peanuts and small crunchy fried fish. Women, with their babies sleeping on their backs, sat gossiping around their calabashes of sour milk. Ojo was amazed to see so many people and so much food in one place. When everyone had gone home, he and his pets scrounged whatever scraps they could from the empty market-place.

That night, Ojo could not sleep. He knew there was no way he was going to let himself starve when there was so much food in the world. The next day, he decided to find out more about the market-place.

During his daily wanderings, he came upon a villager who explained that market days were staggered so that people from other villages could travel back and forth with their goods.

On the very next market day, Ojo, the tortoise and the monkey walked to the palm-grove near the market-place. Ojo checked several palm trees before choosing the one that seemed to have the most leaves. Then, up they climbed. First, the monkey, with the tortoise clinging to its belly, went up the tree. Next, Ojo held on to the slender trunk and, like the monkey, climbed up too. Hidden in the crown of long, feather-like leaves, they watched from the safety of the tree. They marvelled at the men dressed in colourful clothes and the women with beautiful turbans, their bodies glinting with ornaments, trekking to the market with their goods.

By mid morning, the market-place was busy and the drummers beat their drums to announce the arrival of meat from the slaughterhouse. Ojo knew it was time to put his plan into action. He wasn't sure if it would work, for he had never tried magic of this magnitude before, and never on a tree. Still, he closed his eyes, thought of his father, and chanted quietly:

Palm tree, Palm tree,
Shake your roots free
Walk to the market-place
One, two, three.

At the count of three, the tree jiggled its roots out of the palm-grove and began walking towards the market-place. The magic had worked! Ojo could hardly wait to sink his teeth into the sweet flesh of guavas. As the tree wobbled from side to side, Ojo and his pets held on tight to avoid falling.

The women selling sour milk were the first to see the tree. They screamed, alarming the people around them, who dropped their trays, knocked over their stalls, spilled food from their baskets and ran for the safety of their homes. Soon, the palm-grove was once more deserted. Ojo and his pets climbed down and ate until their bellies ached. They also stuffed food in a bag, for they knew there would not be another market for four days. When they had finished, they climbed back the same way and Ojo closed his eyes, thought of his father and chanted:

> *Palm tree, Palm tree*
> *Now you are free,*
> *Walk back to the grove*
> *One, two, three.*

And at the count of three, the tree wobbled back to its spot.

Meanwhile, the frightened villagers went to the chief and told him the strange story. 'Our market has been robbed by a dancing tree!' they wailed.

'Have you lost your brains?' asked the chief. He, of course, didn't believe the story, and this made the

villagers very angry. Seeing how angry they were, he promptly promised to send his advisers to investigate.

Four days later, the same thing happened. This time, the drummers saw the tree first. They drummed vigorously to alert the people and then fled, with the villagers running behind them. Again, the people dropped their trays, spilled their food and knocked down their stalls before escaping to the safety of their homes. The chief's advisers ran the hardest, tripping on their robes.

'It's true! It's true!' they gasped.

'Have you gone crazy?' mocked the chief. He had heard many strange things but never of a dancing tree, and he still thought it was a ridiculous tale. But seeing how upset his people were, he promptly promised to come in person to see this tree for himself.

On the day of the next market, the chief arrived with great pomp and show. His flowing embroidered robe and red hat distinguished him from the people with whom he mingled. By mid morning, the marketplace was full of people, and business was good. This time the chief was the first one to see the palm tree dancing towards the stalls. He was also the first to run away screaming, followed by his advisers and then the panic-stricken villagers.

As soon as the chief arrived back at the village, he rushed to summon all the elders, the wise men, and even a magician from the neighbouring village, to a

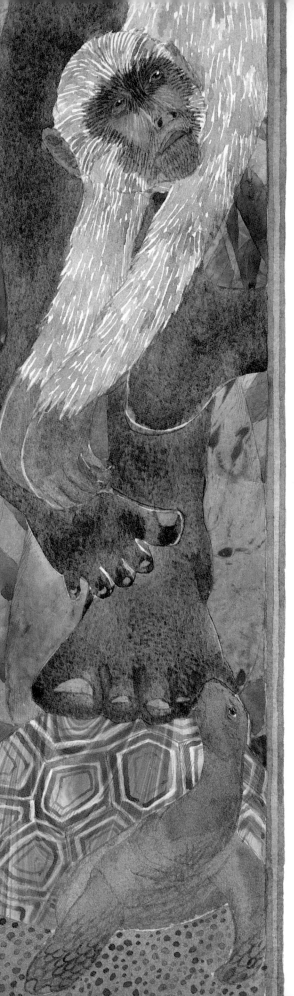

meeting. At the meeting, which lasted two days, they pondered over the problem, and the chief promised a bag of gold to anyone who could come up with a solution. The magician, who was well known for his skills, offered to give it a try.

On the day of the next market, the people began to converge and set up as usual. By mid morning the place was busy. The palm tree came dancing in again, and this time, everyone was waiting for it. They all fled, as was their plan, and the magician remained hidden behind a vegetable stall. What he saw truly amazed him. A boy, a tortoise and a monkey emerged from the tree! He couldn't believe that these three had caused such havoc. Well, well, it was time to teach them a lesson.

While the culprits were busy stuffing food down their throats, the magician crept up and caught the boy by his neck and the monkey by his tail; then he put his foot firmly on top of the tortoise. He held on to them like that until the angry villagers returned with the chief. The villagers kept shouting at the boy and his pets. They wanted the monkey and the tortoise to be killed right away, and Ojo to be given a good thrashing. The chief signalled them to be quiet so he could investigate for himself.

'Who are you?' demanded the chief.

'I am Ojo, Yobachi Baba's son,' said Ojo, trembling with fear.

Ah, the famous Yobachi Baba, the chief thought. If at ten years of age, this boy can make trees dance, surely he has the potential to become a great magician one day.

Handing the bag of gold to the magician, the chief deliberated over the matter no more.

'The tortoise and the monkey will get a good thrashing and Ojo will be raised as my son,' announced the chief.

Ojo hugged the tortoise and the monkey and began to cry. 'Beat me up if you have to, but please don't hurt my pets. It was all my fault. I told them to steal the food because we were hungry,' he cried, between sobs. The villagers looked at each other and felt sorry for Ojo and his pets. They told the chief to forget the punishment. They were happy to have their market-place back and considered themselves lucky that it wasn't the work of the evil spirits. Ojo was delighted with the verdict. It also meant he would never go hungry again.

Ojo grew up to be a great magician like his father. The tortoise and the monkey remained his companions for many years. The palm tree, which was never sent back, took root in the market-place and that's where it stands even today. People of that village believe the spirit of the market-place lives in it and often leave little offerings of food at the foot of the palm tree.

The sycamore fig is an evergreen tree

and it has wide spreading branches.

The fruits are round and grow in great clusters.

The heart-shaped leaves are about five centimetres long,

and the sap from the fig tree is like milky latex.

The leaves of some of the species were used medicinally

to treat coughs and eye disorders

so it is also known as the healing tree.

THE FIG TREE

Jewish

Pinchow was a small Polish town with dark houses and many narrow streets, most of them leading to the town square. It was there, in the square, that people gathered after work, to exchange stories of their lives and whisper about their neighbours. The people of Pinchow were poor, but no matter how hard they worked, baking bread, mending shoes, tailoring clothes and butchering meat, there was never enough food on the table at the end of the day.

In the town lived a shoemaker, named Hershel, a master of his trade. If it had been possible, he would have made new shoes all day. But in a place where people worried about having enough bread for their next Sabbath, they could not possibly afford new shoes. So Hershel had resigned himself to simple repair work. From morning till evening, he put patches of leather on the holes that poverty had made.

Hershel and his wife, Mirka, had a son named Mendel. He was young and handsome but showed no obvious signs of cleverness. He wasn't exactly a fool, although Hershel was tempted to call him that from time to time. Hershel knew Mendel would not conquer a kingdom or marry a princess, but being his father, he worried about his son's future. He wanted him to settle into a good trade and marry a sensible girl who would take care of him. One day, when Hershel could no longer watch his son idle away his time, he called to him, 'Son, you cannot spend your life doing nothing. It is time you went out into the world to seek your own fortune.'

Then Hershel sat Mendel down, measured his feet and set about making the strongest pair of sandals he had ever created. When they were finished, Hershel packed up the sandals, an extra set of clothes and some food for Mendel's journey. 'Come back when you have made something of your life,' said Hershel, giving his son a hundred zlotys from his savings.

Mendel had no idea what he was looking for, but he set out on his journey. He walked through small towns, which resembled Pinchow in many ways. Sometimes he was lucky and a Jewish family would invite him for Sabbath. At other times he spent the night at a small inn or a synagogue. Many weeks passed, and soon Mendel's wanderings began taking him into a land that seemed very different from his own. Here the earth was covered with lush, green trees, and the sun beat down more warmly. Feeling too hot in his coat and boots, Mendel packed them up in his bag and decided

to try on the new sandals his father had made. And what handsome sandals they were! Mendel walked and walked until he was so tired that he decided to take a nap. He stopped by a tree, placed his bundle underneath his head and went to sleep.

While he slept, Mendel had a strange dream. In it, he saw a girl crying in a dark room, her bed littered with figs and leaves. When Mendel awoke, he found he had a clear memory of the dream. This seemed strange to him because on most days, he couldn't even remember what he had eaten for lunch, and to recall a dream was quite out of the ordinary. Standing up, Mendel closely examined the tree under which he had slept. It was a massive tree, with wide spreading branches, and was laden with figs, growing in great clusters. A fig tree! The leaves and the fruits looked exactly like the ones in his dream. Realising this could not be a coincidence, Mendel quickly picked some figs and leaves from the tree's branches. He stripped off some bark and a thick, milky sap came out like tears and dried as pellets in his hands. He packed the leaves, figs, bark and sap pellets in his bag, and began his trek to the next town.

As he walked, Mendel found himself understanding the world around him in a new way. He discovered that, for the first time, there were real thoughts in his head and he suddenly felt clever. It must be the sandals, he said to himself, again and again. What he didn't know was that a heart-shaped leaf from the magical fig tree had stuck itself to the sole of his sandal and was responsible for his growing wisdom.

The next town Mendel came upon was much bigger — in fact he had never seen anything like it, for it was the capital of a kingdom. The town square was enormous and there were lots of shops. He noticed that every shop window had a sign on it:

WANTED — A CURE FOR BLINDNESS!

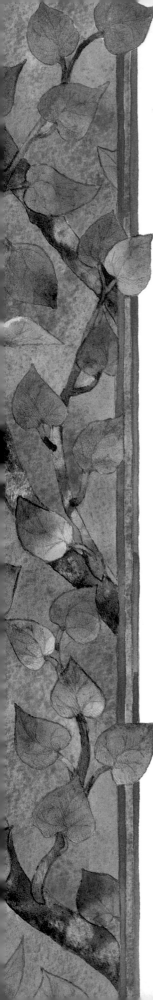

Curious about this message, Mendel walked into a bakery and asked why there were signs everywhere. He was told that the king's only daughter had been struck blind as a result of a mysterious fever. The greatest doctors in the land had been summoned, but no one could cure her.

'Take me to your king,' said Mendel urgently.

The people of the town took him to the palace where anyone who promised a cure was welcome. There he was led to a chamber where the beautiful princess sat in a huge bed, crying. Mendel knew exactly what to do for her. He asked to use the royal kitchen, where he prepared a concoction of the sap pellets, leaves and bark of the fig tree. As he poured the mixture into the princess's eyes, Mendel gave strict instructions that she should remain in total darkness for two days. Not only the king, but also the entire kingdom prayed. On the third day, the princess opened her eyes and cried, 'I can see, Father!' They were the sweetest words the king had heard for a long, long time. He was so overjoyed that he called the royal treasurer to bring five bags of gold to reward Mendel. But thanks to the fig leaf that was still stuck on his sandal, Mendel was wise enough to decline the reward. 'Your Highness,' he said, 'the cure may have a price for you, but for me it is priceless.' Such profound words so pleased the king that he made Mendel his minister.

Mendel served as the king's minister for several months, and he continued to astound the king with his ideas, his clever ways of solving problems, and his witty observations.

'What is the secret of your wisdom?' the king couldn't help asking one day.

'The secret is in my sandals,' confessed Mendel, pointing down towards his dusty feet. The sandals looked quite dirty, for Mendel never cleaned them, afraid of washing away their magic.

'What do you mean?' demanded the king, offended by the answer.

'It's true,' said Mendel, and he went on to narrate the dream he had right after wearing them — the dream that led to the cure of the princess.

'Can I have your sandals, then?' asked the king.

Thanks to the leaf still stuck on his sandals, Mendel knew to decline. The king even offered him ten bags of gold but Mendel shook his head.

But the king was desperate. Finally, he declared, 'I offer you my daughter in marriage.'

To Mendel the offer was tempting indeed. 'I would be truly honoured to marry your beautiful daughter,' he said, 'but it would cause me great grief if I were not able to provide her with the luxuries she is so used to.'

'Then I will also give you half my kingdom,' announced the king.

Half a kingdom? Mendel scratched his head. Certainly, he wouldn't be acting very wisely if he were to pass up such a generous offer.

'As you wish, sire,' Mendel proclaimed, closing the deal.

The delighted king signalled his servants to remove the sandals from Mendel's feet, but Mendel stopped them. 'Not so soon!' he cried. 'Just wait a few more weeks.' And it was decided that the king would receive the sandals only after Mendel had married his new bride.

Preparations for a grand wedding began. While the palace was bustling with activity, one of the king's ministers became fiercely jealous. Why should a stranger claim half a kingdom while he, who had turned grey serving the king, got nothing, he wondered. He decided to try turning the king against Mendel, saying: 'How can you believe his wisdom comes from his sandals? It is ridiculous.' The king thought about it and agreed that yes, it was difficult to believe, so he posed the same question to Mendel.

'Well then, you can put the sandals to the test,' replied Mendel with great confidence. 'Ask me a question that no human being on earth could possibly answer, and I will prove to you by answering correctly that my sandals are responsible for my wisdom.'

The jealous minister consulted many wise men of the kingdom, and together they came up with a question that they all agreed would be impossible to answer.

That evening everyone gathered, and the king asked Mendel the designated question, 'How many stars are there in the sky?'

Mendel stepped out of the palace, looked up at the sky, did some silent calculations and came back with an answer. 'Eighty thousand, nine hundred and sixty seven,' he reported.

'How can you be so precise?' asked the jealous minister.

'You can count for yourself,' said Mendel, shrugging his shoulders. The minister felt sheepish because he wouldn't dare attempt such a monumental task, even if it were to prove Mendel wrong. But the king was delighted, and he bestowed half the kingdom on Mendel, who sent for his poor parents to come and attend his wedding.

Hershel and Mirka were overjoyed to be reunited with their son and rejoiced in his incredible fortune. After the wedding ceremony was over, Mendel finally handed his sandals to the king. The king took one look at them and instructed his servants to wash them thoroughly. Of course, the servants cleaned the sandals so rigorously that they even washed the leaf away!

Upon losing his sandals, Mendel became a simpleton again, but luckily for him, the clever princess managed the affairs of the kingdom. When the king put on the sandals, he felt no wiser than he already was, but it would have been quite foolish to admit that, so he just kept quiet. And since no one ever talked about it, no one ever found out the secret of the magic leaf from the fig tree.

The pomegranate tree is a small tree,
which grows up to a height of seven metres.
It has shiny foliage and a long flowering season.
The interior is filled with taut sacs full of flavour,
The fruit has a tough leathery skin.
and in each sac is a seed.
The trunk is covered by a reddish-brown bark.
The branches are stiff and spiny.
The wood from the tree is mostly used to make walking sticks.

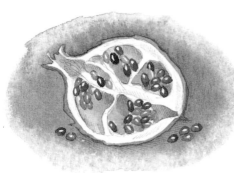

THE POMEGRANATE TREE
Moroccan

Long ago, there lived a tribe of Berbers in Asni, a village in the heart of the Moroccan desert. For as far as the eye could see there was nothing but silent wilderness — a wasteland of sand and rock, dotted with sparse and prickly vegetation.

During the day, the sun beat down on the mud and straw houses. Water was scarce. The closest oasis was half an hour's walk, if the mule that carried the water bag could be persuaded to walk at a fast pace. Needless to say, life was harsh for the people of Asni and harsher still for their animals.

Now, in Asni there was a young boy named Aamir, who lived with his parents and his grandmother. Since there was no school in the village, and Aamir was too young to learn a trade, he spent his days roaming around, playing with his friends and teasing the mules. His only task was to accompany his mother to the oasis once a day. While they were there, his mother would fetch the water, and Aamir would graze their goats on the tamarisk bushes that grew in abundance nearby.

At night, Aamir loved to sleep next to his grandmother, who regaled him with stories of sultans, princesses, djinn and afreets, the spirits of the underworld. '*Kan ma kan*,' she would begin. Once there was and once there wasn't. That's all Aamir would need to hear before he'd be drawn into the world of the story.

One day, as Aamir played inside his house, he heard the sound of crying coming from outside. He looked out of the window to see his friend's mother wailing into the arms of some of the other village women. 'My son, my Salim is missing,' she cried out again and again. 'One minute he was near the oasis, the next minute he was gone,' she howled.

As was their custom when anyone was in trouble, the villagers banded together to help Salim's mother. The men searched for any signs of the missing boy. The women lit candles, said prayers and kept a close watch on all the other children.

A few days later, a similar incident happened near the oasis and another child went missing. Then another, and another. A great sadness fell over the village. Mothers tied amulets and talismans on their children's arms and people spoke in hushed whispers. Aamir was the saddest of all. Many of his playmates were gone, including his best friend, Jamal.

Eleven children disappeared, one by one. Some of the villagers thought that this must be the work of a djinn. Aamir's grandmother knew all about djinn, and the trouble they could cause. Every night, Aamir begged her to tell him more about them.

'Djinn,' she said, 'can be difficult to deal with. They can take any shape — of man or woman or animal — but they have a weakness. They aren't very clever. They live in palaces filled with silver and gold, and are easily flattered because they love to be pampered and groomed. Sometimes, they even fall in love with humans.'

His grandmother's words gave Aamir courage, and he had an idea about how he might rescue the missing children. He began saving figs, dates and roasted chickpeas for the journey he was planning.

One morning, before the crack of dawn, with only a sack filled with dried food and a small goatskin water bag, Aamir crept out of the house

and made his way to the oasis. Not expecting to meet anyone at that hour of the day, he was surprised to see a strange woman dressed in black robes. Shaking like a leaf on a tree, he moved closer, pretending to fill his water bag. When he dared to look up, he shivered with fright, for what he saw was a human face with eyes of burning coal. A djinnia! One glimpse of the terrible creature and his blood ran cold.

Before he had time to think of a plan, he found himself falling under her spell. He felt compelled to follow her, but had enough wit to drop the dried fruits to mark his trail. When he ran out of figs and dates, he began dropping chickpeas.

As the day wore on, Aamir became tired by the long journey. He found himself dragging his feet along path after path. Finally, the djinnia

brought him to a dilapidated old house. Outside it grew a magnificent pomegranate tree, and Aamir felt himself coming out of his trance as he gazed at it. The tree was small and had thick, shiny leaves and many beautiful blossoms. Its spiky branches drooped with the weight of round, red pomegranates. Suddenly, Aamir remembered what his grandmother had once told him — that the pomegranate tree has special powers in its twigs, and is the only tree that grows in paradise. Rightly so, thought Aamir, pausing briefly to admire it.

He followed the djinnia inside, expecting to find walls made of gold and silver. His grandmother had said that djinn lived in palaces, but this house seemed poorer than his own. The djinnia locked the door behind them and led him into another room, bigger and darker than the one they had just passed through. On the mud floor were mats, a heap of pomegranates and a neat row of cages, with sorry looking parrots inside. Aamir counted eleven in all. He watched in fearful fascination as the djinnia unlocked the cages, and with a wand she pulled out of her robes, turned all eleven parrots into children. And there they stood — from head to toe — Salim, Maaja, Najim, Zara and oh, even his best friend, Jamal. Aamir wanted to cry out his name and give him a hug, but he managed to restrain himself. How weak and tired his friends looked, as if they hadn't been fed for days.

So far the djinnia had not spoken a word, but suddenly she turned to Aamir. 'Boy,' she shouted, 'crack open the fruit and shell out the sacs!' Aamir shuddered as he sat down with his friends; with their little fingers they began cracking the pomegranates. They split the bitter tissue inside and out of the tightly packed compartments, took the sacs that were deep red like gemstones, and put them in a wooden bowl. As they were working, the djinnia disappeared through another door. Aamir tried to

speak to his friends but the djinnia came back, hitting a stick on the floor. 'Work faster, you mules!' she cried and disappeared again. Later, she came back to collect the wooden bowl once more.

Aamir knew it was time to make his move. 'Let me carry the bowl for you, my lady,' he said, most respectfully. He hoped that, like all djinn, she would respond to good manners. And she did. She let him follow her through a secret door and down forty stairs into a cave. What Aamir saw there nearly made him drop the bowl. 'Ya, Yimma!' he exclaimed under his breath, as he laid eyes on the dazzling riches displayed before him. There were chairs of hammered silver, cushions of silk, kilims all over the floor and jewels spilling out of brass pots.

Aamir placed the bowl filled with pomegranate sacs on a table and before the djinnia had time to dismiss him, he offered to make her some mint tea. 'I make the best tea in Morocco,' he boasted politely, trying hard not to stare at the treasures around him.

The djinnia was charmed by Aamir's courtesy. As she reclined on her bed, sipping the syrupy mint tea, Aamir offered to clip her discoloured and ugly toenails. He remembered from his grandmother's stories that djinn liked to be groomed. He rubbed turmeric paste on the boils on her feet. He recoiled at massaging her straggly, grey hair but did it anyway. As the days passed, he even got used to looking at her burning eyes. At night, she would turn all the children except Aamir back into parrots. 'They are safer in their cages,' she cackled, 'but you are safer here with me.'

Slowly, the djinnia began to trust Aamir, and let him watch as she dipped the pomegranate sacs into a magic potion that turned them instantly into garnets, the beautiful gemstones of Morocco. She even let him string them into necklaces.

One day, the djinnia announced that she was going to the souk, to sell the necklaces she had made. She disguised herself as a Bedouin woman and, before she left, Aamir jumped towards her. 'Please let me carry the load for you, my lady,' he said politely, and the djinnia agreed.

As they approached the souk, the smell of fresh bread was like a whiff of paradise to Aamir, who was sick with longing for sesame cakes and couscous. The souk itself was a busy place. The shopkeepers had their stalls of melons, olives and spices. Mountains of mint were covered with wet sacks to keep them fresh. Barbers were shaving old men's beards and fortune-tellers were spinning glorious futures for the poor people. The dentist with the pliers had the biggest crowd around him. He had a display of all the teeth he had ever extracted in his life.

The djinnia set up her display of necklaces near the snake charmer, and by the end of the day she had sold them all.

After their day at the souk, Aamir decided to charm the djinnia into spending more and more time in the cave downstairs. In her presence, he would bang the stick on the floor, shouting at his friends to work faster. But when she was sleeping, he fed them with stolen food and kissed their bruised hands. Every week, he accompanied her to the souk. Things went on this way for a month, until Aamir had earned her trust. Now it was time to make his next move. While the djinnia slept one afternoon, Aamir crept outside and broke off some twigs from the pomegranate tree. With a cage in one hand and the branches in the other, he went down the forty stairs to where she slept. He tiptoed towards her and thrust the branches into her face and over her body. The magic twigs grasped on to the djinnia, imprisoning her beneath them. Then Amir stole the wand from her robes and turned her into a parrot, threw her in the cage and locked it.

Aamir quickly filled a bag with as many gemstones as he could and went upstairs to free his friends. They could hardly believe their good fortune and were filled with admiration for Aamir's bravery. They laughed with delight when Aamir told them that he had turned the djinnia into a parrot. On their way out, Aamir reverently touched the pomegranate tree to acknowledge the gift of freedom it had bestowed upon them. Then following the trail of the chickpeas, figs and dates, he brought them all to the oasis and from there to the village.

There was much rejoicing when the children
returned, and the sheikh threw a big feast in honour of
Aamir. But Aamir was just happy to be back. He had
missed his mother and father but, most of all, he had
missed his grandmother.

'*Kan ma kan*,' he began, as he lay down next to her.
It was his turn to be the storyteller. Once there was and
once there wasn't. And he told her the story of the
djinnia and the pomegranate tree.

Sources

THE CYPRESS TREE

This story is adapted from Isabelle C. Chang's retelling in *Tales from Old China* (Norton, New York, 1969) and embodies the universal belief that trees belong to everyone.

THE KAPOK TREE

The seeds of this story came from Dorothy Sharpe Carter's *The Enchanted Orchard and other Folktales of Central America* (Harcourt Brace Jovanovich, Inc., San Diego, 1973), but the story itself was inspired by the rainforest.

THE CHESTNUT TREE

The basis of this story is the gentle friendship between a girl and a chestnut tree. It's a variation of the folktale found in Miroslav Novak's *Fairy Tales from Japan* (Hamlyn, London 1970).

THE CHERRY BLOSSOM TREE

This story is about a friendship between the majestic cherry tree and the poor kusa grass that grows around it. It is based on a Jataka tale found in Frederick & Audrey Hyde-Chambers' *Tibetan Folktales* (Shambhala Publications, Inc., Boston, 1981).

THE PALM TREE

Trees can fill us with awe even though they are rooted in one place. If they were to move and dance around, they would probably fill us with terror. The version found in Barbara K. Walker's *The Dancing Palm Tree and other Nigerian Folktales* (Texas Tech University Press, Lubbock, 1990) has a tortoise as its central character.

THE FIG TREE

This story grew out of a brief anecdote (entitled 'The Tree of Knowledge') mentioned in Leonard Wolf's *Yiddish Folktales*, (Pantheon Books, New York, 1988) edited by Beatrice Silverman Weinreich.

THE POMEGRANATE TREE

The story, as such, does not exist in Arab folklore. It was the fascinating account of the djinn, ghouls, and afreets in Inea Bushnaq's *Arab Folktales* (Pantheon Books, New York, 1996) that inspired me to write about the tree that bears my favourite fruit.